GREENLIGHT

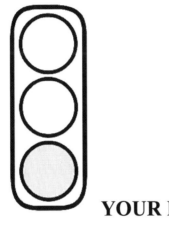

YOUR LIFE

Awakening Your Higher Self

BRIAN GERMAIN

ISBN: 097762771-3
ISBN-13: 9780977627714
Library of Congress Control Number: 2008908993

This book is dedicated to my fourth grade teacher, Mrs. Donatt, my Mom and my loving wife, Laura:

You were right.
I do need someone to light a fire under my butt to get me going.

So it turns out, that someone can be me.

Contents

5

Preface

One of the many hats I wear is that of an advanced parachuting instructor. I videotape my students' approaches and landings, and discuss their performance. Before I debrief them, I warn them of a few things, which I will now relate to you, the reader of this book.

I am here to help. I will be direct and honest, and tell you what you most need to hear. Please do not get offended by the degree to which I am straight with you. If I am to do my job, I must tell you the truth.

Sometimes the truth stirs up our defenses, and since we are not accustomed to teachers being so direct, we attribute their comments to some ulterior motive. This leads us to question the fundamental validity of the instruction. That is just our insecurity talking, but it can redirect the course of our experience. If we let our questioning undermine the aspects of the information that are beneficial to us, we deflect the positive impact that information might have on our lives. If we are to change, if we are to expand, we must remain open to anything and everything that helps us along to the next level. All I am asking you to do is try it on.

So, as I say to all my students, you must remember that whatever it is that I am pointing out that may need changing, it is not who you are, it is just what you did. Do not hold onto the way things have been. It is already the past, and your future is wide open to infinite possibility.

I honestly mean that. I have witnessed thousands of people make transitions to a higher level of prowess and joy in their skydiving skills. I know it is possible. I believe that we are equally capable of making such a transition in our lives in general. Through my honest belief in the possibility of the miraculous healing epiphany that will greenlight your life in the very near future, I am actually increasing the likelihood of this happening. I believe in the possibility of the enlightenment of all beings. If this is to happen, however, you must do your part.

You must believe it is possible.

*Further, you must believe
that this has already happened,
and that you are already enlightened.*

Part One

Beginning Again

When the words "Greenlight Your Life" hit me square in the forehead, I wrote them on a piece of paper in big magic-marker letters, and drew a traffic light above them. I put my name on the rough cover idea to make it a bit more real to me as an intention; to remind me that I needed to write this book.

Interestingly, I didn't color the traffic light green right away. I left it in black-and-white for months. I realized that there were things I needed to do before I myself felt I was in a "state of greenlight." I couldn't give myself permission to open this new chapter of my life until I had gotten my whole house in order, so to speak.

So I worked on the many areas of my life that needed completion, working to shed my identification with my addictive patterns of thought and behavior, and dreaming of a better future. Meanwhile the drawing of the traffic light sat there on the table, colorless, staring up at me every day, building in expectation, building in the refinement of what that meant to me.

I realized that part of the reason why I hesitated to upgrade my life to the status of greenlight was that I was afraid. I feared the responsibilities that such a life would entail. I was afraid to change the way I had been living. I was afraid that my life would require more effort if I allowed myself to actually try harder. It has been said that we are more afraid of our light than we are of our darkness. I believe this to be true. Nevertheless, if we do not change the way we are living and thinking, we cannot expect our lives to change for the better. We must break the inertia of the way things have been if we are to reach a new level of fulfillment and happiness.

When we decide to greenlight some aspect of our lives, or every aspect of our lives, we enter into a state of movement. The kinetic expression of our will—envisioning where we want to go and what we want to do, and doing it—is the most enjoyable of all human experiences. When we switch the greenlight on, we become more alive.

Are you in school? Do that. Get into it. Find a way to love it. Seize the opportunity to learn everything you ever wanted to learn. Do you have a job? Do it with your full attention. Try to do your job better. If you think you're already doing that, try even harder. Even if this particular job is not where you are ultimately headed, your life will get better simply because of your commitment to pay attention to your world and to do your very best. In short, whatever you are doing, do it better.

You must transfer your awareness from one action to the next, never allowing yourself to fall into the trap of half-hearted involvement in your actions. The thought that can enliven us more than any other is the following realization:

Wake up, you're not dead yet!

Many people live out their lives without ever truly confronting death. They successfully avoid serious danger and therefore never tap into the great source of renewed perspective that occurs upon the realization of the moment of death.

As a professional skydiver and parachute test pilot, I have been fortunate enough to confront death on a fairly regular basis. There have been many moments in my life in which I have genuinely asked the question: "Am I about to die?" Although there is no more terrifying thought, the awakening such a realization brings is the most powerful of all pivot-points. I hope all people experience this at least once in a lifetime.

When you think you are about to die, it changes you. Perhaps you already know what I am talking about. As soon as this thought is entertained, your entire existence looks different. Many of the things that you had been taking so seriously now fade into the background, while others become much more important to you. Things that you wished you had said or done scream out at you for completion, and the big picture of your life comes into perspective.

What if you found out that you only had one year to live? What would you do with your final months? What would be most important to you? Would you finally write that book that you have been thinking about writing for years? More importantly, how would your life look in comparison to what you originally wanted to do? Are you the person you wanted to become?

What if you learned you were going to die one hour from now—what would you think about your life in *that* case? What would you do? Would you call someone to tell them that you love them? Would you call someone to tell them that you are sorry or to forgive them? Would you feel that you had brought out the essential aspects of who you are in the life you have lived?

Imagine now that you are confronted with the reality of your death within the next five minutes. Accept it. It is about to be over. Ponder that for a moment. Sit with it. It's over.

Imagine now that you have been granted a second chance to live. You have been given a fresh new perspective on your life, and the opportunity to use it. How would that affect your thoughts, actions, and dreams for the future?

I have been given this gift repeatedly, as my life flashed before my eyes and then was handed back to me. I now wish to give you this gift. Life is not a certainty; your continued existence is a gift of unimaginable proportions.

Do not waste it.

Newsflash: You really *are* going to die. It may happen today, tomorrow or in fifty years from now. Use whatever time you have left to do things that have meaning. Create closure with the past and make peace with it. Let go of your suffering. Appreciate your life as it is. Love every minute of it.

Greenlighting your life is about using the power of this perspective to infuse your path with meaning, so that you can create a life truly worth living. Once in a while, you need to be like a prairie dog and pop your head up so that you can take in the broader perspective on things. Once you get your priorities straight, you will awaken within you a completely different perspective from the mundane one you have lived with up to now.

Celebrate the fact that you are alive!

Faced with the task of processing all the complexity of our daily lives, and carrying out all of the things that are required of us, it is easy to delude ourselves that our life's end is far away in the distant future. We do not consider the impermanence of it all because it scares us too much even to think about it. The truth is, the *absolute* end of our existence is still very much in question, but the inevitable end of our specific lives, our bodies, and our story, is certainly going to reach a state of termination. It is this ending to which I refer. It is the realization of this ending that can return us to the original, inspired intention of who we truly are.

Your work here is not yet complete. It never will be. The process of revealing your character in the world is still in a state of becoming as you add to your vision of who you are. You must allow yourself to develop more awareness of your deeper ideals, and act upon your most powerful emotions, the ones that help you to see what these ideals are. You must rediscover yourself.

When you realize what it is that you want to do with your life, the epiphany will come packaged in huge emotion. The emotion will be so powerful, in fact, that it will cloud your way at times. Do not let that worry you; it's just the process by which we find truth. We must look beyond the thunderous clouds of emotion, and get on with the progression of becoming who we really are.

Emotion is our way of discovering what it is we truly love and hate. Both kinds of information are essential to a happy life. This means that we must allow ourselves to experience emotion, both positive and negative, so that we can realize how we really feel, and who we really are. This means you will transcend your current conditions through the heat of your most powerful feelings. All you will ever find in your mundane, unemotional experiences is more of the same. If you want to live a truly extraordinary life, you have to allow yourself to experience extraordinary feelings.

You have two parts:
your emotions
and your intellect.

If you do not listen to both,
you are not a
complete human being.

Sanity requires balance.

🎱 Turning Emotion into Motion

I have spent much of my adult life studying the topic of fear and how it affects us. My initial conclusion, one that I preached for many years, was that fear, quite simply, is bad for us. Intense emotion, I concluded, robs the brain of its access to those necessary logical functions that provide us with constructive responses to any given situation. I have seen the catastrophic effects of full-blown fear, and there appear to be no redeeming qualities to the overt expression of this and other negative emotions.

After careful consideration and observation of my own experience, I now see that I was only half-correct. Emotion, if allowed to carry us without the guidance of logical thought processes, wisps us away to a set of thoughts and behaviors that cannot easily be controlled until the emotion is gone. Furthermore, we cannot see our way out of the problem that has led us to this negative emotional experience while we are under the influence of the emotion. We are in the wrong mindset for creating solutions.

From the perspective of fear, anger and other negative emotional experiences, I stand by my original conclusions. Allowing negative emotions to control our actions cannot lead us to where we want to go, nor is it the most effective tool for avoiding what we do not want. This is not a constructive state of mind, and it can therefore only create destruction.

However, I have also come to realize that emotions can speak to us in ways that logic cannot. Emotions provide us with the essential information that empowers us to make more profound changes in our lives than logic can ever hope to do. The trouble is, the information comes to us packaged in an onslaught of defensive thinking that is contractive. That is to say, it is limiting, and assumes that the worst-case scenario is on the verge of playing out. At the very least, the thoughts and expectations that fear and negative emotions lead me to never seem to include the best-case scenario, thus significantly reducing the chances that it will occur.

As a skydiving instructor, I have noticed that excessive fear tends to cause my students to make rash decisions that often result in injuries. Or, even worse, they do absolutely nothing, which is a bad choice when there is a planet racing up at you. It is therefore reasonable to assert that fear is something that we need to mitigate. Finding ways to counteract negative emotions is therefore paramount in our success as human beings.

In my experience, the fastest way out of intense negative emotions is by letting go of thought altogether. I have found huge success with the use of meditation and other grounding practices to help my students calm down and allow their physiological experience to relax so that their minds can begin to work rationally again. By emptying the mind of all thought, we are less driven by the momentum of the emotion. From there, we are open to better possibilities. The better we are at the process of letting go of thought, the sooner we can get back to the job of being the champion of the best-case scenario.

Although I still hold that this process is essential to avoiding the negative side effects of intense emotional experiences, I have also recognized that without emotion, we are not complete. While striving to transcend our negative thinking, we must also remember to explore what the emotion was trying to tell us.

We come to the realizations that guide our lives through many different processes. Often this involves the kind of careful, methodical appraisal that can only occur within the realm of calm assessment. Nevertheless, an equally important aspect of the process requires the nebulous workings of emotional thinking to bring us to the realization of how we truly feel and what we really want.

Our emotions often direct us to what our reason would have us avoid. When our rational left-brains govern our thought processes, we often fail to consult our inner wisdom, gleaned from the broader perspective of our deeper awareness of what we truly believe in. We must therefore learn to blend our "sane," reason-based thoughts with the wordless feelings of the emotional mind.

This is the stickiest zone of human experience. It would be much easier to teach that emotion is messy, irrational, and should be avoided at all costs. This oversimplification leads us to throw the baby out with the bathwater. Clearly, there are emotional processes that are destructive, and lead us to make things worse by acting on impulse. However, some emotional thoughts give us the power to reject what we hate, and to create experiences that we love. When we feel this kind of authentic inspiration, we must allow it to fill us with power and purpose. Then we must turn this feeling into action. This is the difference between avoiding emotion and using it to our benefit.

We must get our hands dirty. The clean feeling of an emotionless existence is impotent. If we are to step beyond the fear of our emotions to become extraordinary human beings who actually do what we came here to do, we must allow ourselves to acknowledge the wisdom of our emotions and convert this potential energy into positive kinetic flow. Otherwise, we will be like a boat with its sails down, unable to navigate the world using the power of our passion.

Emotion is complicated, but it makes us who we are. Emotions give us information about who we are and what we like and dislike. If we dwell upon negative emotions, however, we find ourselves trapped into seeing only problems and obstacles. Only when we deliberately choose to be positive people, and focus on what we want for ourselves, can we begin to use emotion to drive us forward into authentic experience and a life worth living.

What it comes down to is learning how to choose which thoughts to follow and develop, and which ones to leave aside. When we can do this, we become focused in our efforts, and steadfast in our direction. Once this happens, there is a shift, and we find ourselves living the life that we always wanted to live more of the time than ever before. When you harness the power of your mind, there is pretty much nothing you cannot do.

🚦Green, Yellow, and Red

Every aspect of your life is in one of three possible states: green light (go), yellow light (pause), or red light (stop). By realizing the "color" of each of our life experiences, we can decide how we are going to upgrade our status to one of mobility. Furthermore, we will be able to see what is holding us back.

The areas of your life that are moving forward into full expression can be said to be in a state of green light. You are actively engaged in the processes that bring this particular thing into being. You have become this thing, this role, because you no longer resist its expression. You allow it to be in motion.

Other things are stunted, so to speak, in their growth toward fruition. They are possibilities that have not yet become reality, due either to incomplete execution, or incomplete commitment to the actions that would have allowed this possibility to occur. Due to fear in some form, you have not surrendered to walking this new path; therefore you hesitate and resist allowing yourself to have whatever it is that you want for yourself.

This can be something material like a new car or home, or a more ethereal goal like a meaningful friendship or romantic love. Regardless of the context, we all have aspects of ourselves that are still waiting to be actualized, i.e., in a state of "yellow light."

Other things that you want to create for yourself are far from becoming reality, despite your intense yearning for them to come into existence. This is the condition of "red light." It is these things that you surround with the most resistance, in the form of fear and its cognitive counterpart, negative thinking. You spend your time complaining about the absence of this thing or condition, rather than beginning the process of bringing it into being.

When you continue to focus your mind on the absence of the object of your desires by dwelling on the current state of affairs, you are negating your own dream. If you are to become effective in creating your life the way you want it, you must learn how to transcend your negative thoughts and dedicate your time and energy toward the realization of this particular set of goals. You must genuinely believe that this possibility can occur, and focus on *making* it occur.

For many reasons, what you repeat in your mind becomes what you experience. If you linger on the current moment with all its shortcomings, you are not working to change things. You are recognizing what it is that you do not want, but you are not doing anything to create an alternative. The process of bringing new things into the world begins with the invention of an alternate set of possibilities.

The state of red light is what the Buddhists call the "Hungry Ghost" realm. We know what it is that we want, but we feel powerless to obtain it. Like a ghost, hungry for physical experience, we are unable to attain what we desire, and are therefore stuck in a persistent state of suffering. The reason for our immobility is not the outside world creating limitations for us; it is our own projected limitations that hold us back. There is almost always a way to get whatever it is that we want. We just need to envision it clearly enough to make it happen. If we cannot express what we want, there is very little likelihood that it will come to be.

Even if by chance we get what we have dreamt of getting, if we are not ready to receive it, we will not be able to live it. This is ultimately how we evade our dreams. We stuff our dream into a bottle and cast it away. But when a ship finally comes to rescue us, we are not ready to be rescued, because we are off hiding in a cave or busy doing other things. If you are to live as your higher self, you must be ready for things to go well.

Be prepared for the best-case scenario.

⦂ From Red to Green

In order to transform the color of the light surrounding your dreams, you must recognize that sometimes the light is red for a good reason. There are incomplete aspects about the thing you are giving birth to that need doing. You must do them, whatever they are, if you are to move forward in the creation of your mind-child.

On the other hand, many of our red lights are purely neurotic in origin, fueled by fear and negative habits of thought that prevent the current state of affairs from changing. You may have unconsciously sent up a red flag that blocks the realization of your dream. You may be carrying thoughts and behaviors that are toxic to its realization; even though you may not be fully aware that you are snuffing out the fire of your vision. This is where you must start.

Turning on the green light must always begin with turning off all the red lights.

You must clean up your house, literally and figuratively. If your toilets are dirty, your life energy will be affected, because you do not feel good about your home. If the dishes are piled up in your sink, you will not be able to cook yourself a beautiful meal that nourishes your soul and prepares you for your next adventure or insight. Likewise, you must clean your consciousness of all negative beliefs and patterns of self-disgust, so that you can begin to connect with the self-affirming affection that lights up your life.

The process of turning off your red lights requires you to notice the nature of your habitual thoughts and actions. What will it feel like to reside in the state of completion with your dream? Is your current way of thinking congruous with the feeling of your ultimate goal? Are you acting as if your dream is actually going to come true? The only way to be in a position to meet up with your dream when it is ready to reach culmination is to be in a state of positive expectation. Otherwise, when the signs begin to come through that your vision is starting to take shape, you will not be in a place in your life in which you are ready to act when action is necessary.

You must know what you want. When you hold your aspiration clearly enough, and avoid thoughts and actions that inhibit its coming into being, you are on your way. The original essence of a heartfelt vision is never the problem. The problem is your subsequent negation of the vision through thoughts that prevent it from unfolding.

We all do it. We have a thought that fires us up and we allow ourselves to develop it for a time. We begin to feel what it would be like to have this thing come true, and we love that feeling. This is the original essence that will propel the dream through environments that do not remotely resemble the dream itself. The process of creating will always involve holding fast to our intention amidst chaos and conflicting circumstances.

The dreamer's most important job is to hold on to the intention, despite indications from the current state of affairs that this has not yet come into being. You must be patient. You must remain in touch with your invention of thought if you are to be its number one proponent. You must hold it in your mind as if its eventual actualization were an absolute certainty, and you must allow the specific events that contribute to this process to unfold. You must get out of its way, mainly by ceasing to resist, no matter what form your resistance takes. You must let yourself succeed.

"If you are hunting for Moby Dick, bring tartar sauce."
-Dale Carnegie

From Red to Yellow

There are times in our lives when we feel so lost and stuck that we have trouble changing the red light all the way to green. Life can present powerful, overwhelming challenges. Sometimes the only way out of these situations is to reach for something above where you are, even if it is just a tiny bit better than what you are experiencing.

In the absence of clear reasons for hope, sometimes the only thing that can pull us out is our skill of opening our minds to the positive direction; what I call the "General Direction of Up". One of the most powerful life-tools for regaining this perspective is something taught to me by a very wise friend named Abraham. It goes like this:

> "It's getting better,
> it's getting better,
> and it's going to be alright."

When there is no hope left in you, repeating mantras like this can be of huge assistance.

When you consider the possibility that everything is going to be OK, things begin to look different. You have introduced a new direction to your experience, born not of the present situation, but from something that you carry inside you. No matter what is going on, there is always that idea waiting for you.

Amazingly, when you allow yourself to consider that everything will be just fine, it begins to become true for you. It may not happen all at once because we are still wading in the slow quagmire of time, but if you are patient, and you keep repeating the idea in your head that all is well, you begin to see evidence of it.

In a way, deliberately changing one's perspective to a more positive one simply purchases us the power to be patient and wait for things to get better. On the other hand, there is a profound effect to a positive frame of mind that can never be completely explained because it is, in essence, faith.

Where an individual derives their faith from is very personal. You have your own body of experience and wisdom, and you come from a specific lineage of culture in which your personal wisdom makes sense. All you need to do is trust it and you will find that, despite appearances, there is always something better than what you are seeing right now. If you look with the eyes of your higher self, you will see that all is in fact, very, very well.

Reasonable Life-Motto:

Be happy anyway.

Self-Actualization

This is how we realize the big ideas worth greenlighting: We stop. We step outside the flow of our lives and sit down. Once we have stopped, we calm down and ground ourselves. When this happens, we begin to feel good again. We then awaken to whatever is most important to us at that particular moment in time.

Sometimes nothing specific comes to us when we sit down. All we get, then, is a refreshed perspective on things, which, after all, is what we most need to take the next step forward. The state of appreciation is the most refreshing of all feelings. By feeling thankful for what we have, we connect with the feeling that allows us to spring forward into the next expression of who we are and what we want to do.

Sometimes, on the other hand, we receive a specific thought that holds a very important meaning for us. These are the thoughts that show us who we really are. Such thoughts only come when we are in our highest state, and are ultimately what lead us to what we want in life. These thoughts come from the higher self.

*If a thought feels good,
it is compatible with
who you truly are on the inside.*

*It is a reflection of the nature of
your higher self.*

Peace and Happiness

It is true that every human being on the face of the earth has experienced moments of blissful peace. The fact that we are each capable of experiencing this means that we can therefore experience it again. We must simply choose it.

Think of the children's game called "musical chairs." Sometimes the chairs are not all of the same kind. When there is one chair that is more comfortable than the others are, we think, "I hope I get to sit in that one again." If we get the chance, we will do our best to jump back into the comfy chair. By our deliberate effort, we can increase the frequency with which we engage in things that bring us true happiness and peace. All we have to do is remember what we like, and when the opportunity arises, we simply say yes.

Yes happens in the moment. It happens when you are moving through the space of your life, doing whatever you do, while confidently expecting that wonderful experiences are likely to occur. If you look, you will find everything you need, including moments of perfect bliss and the subsequent epiphanies that connect you with yourself.

*You are free to be as happy
as you allow yourself to be.*

🎱 Non-Contingent Enlightenment

Rather than following our desires and addictions around the wheel of craving, striving, and attainment, we can simply take a breath, right now, and let it all go. It can happen in this very moment. All you need to do is decide to let yourself experience it.

Stop.

Relax.

Now.

This moment is perfect for waking up.
All moments are, if you allow yourself to create the space to truly stop and listen to the silence.

Now, return to the Best-Case Scenario.

Let that inspire you into
Meaningful Action.

🞦 Your Vision

The act of creation has two parts: the vision and the action. Your dream has many details that require your attention. If you are to become the most powerful creative force that you can be, you must attend to each exquisitely specific aspect of your dream. Only you can know what these aspects are. It is, after all, *your* dream.

The champion of a vision is not necessarily responsible for all the specific actions that result in the realization of the dream. Your job is to continue to hold the concept in your mind, and simply allow it to occur. There will be work to do, but if the work is done without holding onto the original sensation of the vision, you will be led astray from the ultimate completion of the task. You *see* your vision, yes. But more importantly you *feel* it. If you keep feeling it, it is far more likely to become real.

You have realized many desires, but somehow you have not allowed all of them to come true. It is not too late. You must simply connect with the original feeling of inspiration that you had when you first invested yourself in this dream, and let that feeling guide your action, and your life.

Invest Yourself in Yourself

People put their money on horses they believe will win a race. They put their money in stocks that they believe will increase in value. We invest ourselves in any endeavor that we believe has a good chance of succeeding. This is especially so when we believe that we have enough control over a situation to increase the likelihood of success. Similarly, investing in your moment-to-moment reality with the attitude of best effort provides you with a sense of control, because you are directly connected to the process that is making things happen. You are in control of the situation.

Although we often know exactly where we would like to go, we do not always know how we will get there. That doesn't really matter in the end. What matters is how we act and feel along the way. The universe judges us by the pureness of our intentions, and by our attention to detail in creating what we want. As a horse senses its rider, the world around you knows when you honestly believe in what you are doing. When you believe in yourself, and act without hesitation, things will flow much more easily in the direction of where you want to go.

Often, however, it is actually the realization phase that is our biggest stumbling block. If you realize your vision, you can work toward carrying it out. If, on the other hand, you walk without knowing where you are going, you are sure to end up somewhere you have already been; that or you will end up somewhere you did not want to go. Either way, you will never get what you truly want in life.

This is how we find ourselves feeling like victims. We do not feel conviction about our way, and we get lost. Even when we know what we want, we are never done envisioning the future. Our changing reality requires us to reassess our goals constantly and to get back in touch with the underlying principles that make us who we are.

When you lose touch with who you are, and give up hope that you can become the person you originally wanted to be, you redlight your life. You freeze your growth as a person, and live like a zombie: feeding your addictions, orbiting old habitual patterns of thought, simply getting older. This is not who you were meant to be.

We all get frustrated with our progress from time to time. We lament the difference between what our lives are like and what we want them to be. The trouble is, the more we dwell on the current state of affairs—the deeper we become entrenched in our habitual thinking—the farther we get from our ultimate objective. That, of course, is nothing short of perfect happiness.

The redlight state is one of hopelessness. We feel hopeless because we lose sight of the fact that we have control over our thinking, and over the creative process that manufactures our experience. We must remember that it is the feeling behind our thinking that creates our thoughts, and our thoughts create our reality. If you are addicted to feelings of despair and anguish, you will begin to feel more comfortable with playing the role of the victim. This way of interacting with the world is incongruous with true human nature.

We are not here to suffer. We are not here to toil. We are not here to carry our load as if it were a burden, or to get pushed around by life. We are here to be joyful creators, in control over our wondrous experience here on earth. We are here to tap into our powers of manifestation and bring into the world both what makes sense to us and what makes us feel good.

To believe otherwise is to create a rift between your inner and outer selves. Only by creating can a person truly live in his or her own personal heaven. This is so because anyone else's picture of heaven was not conceived in your specific consciousness, and will not resonate with you on your deepest level. Only through the process of creation, when your inner and outer realities are in harmony, will you experience true happiness.

You Are a Creator

If you are feeling unhappy,
unfulfilled,
lacking the essential energy
to move forward,
it is because you have not been yourself:

You have not been creating.
You have been subsisting.

If you want to feel alive,
You must dream

And then
you must make your dreams into reality.

This is who you are.

You have forgotten something. I do not know what it is, but you do. The only way you will figure out what you need to do to greenlight your life is to sit on your own butt, and wake up.

You have forgotten that you wanted to take a break, a real break, not a half-relaxed moment, defined by its content rather than by its emptiness. You forgot that you wanted to sit down on a rock and just hang out with yourself, and allow yourself the profound sense of relief that you have been withholding for a better moment.

Do it now.

Do not read another word until you put the book down, take a walk to a quiet place, and have a seat for fifteen minutes. You need to clear your head if you want to awaken to who you are.

Go.

Now.

What did you find out?

Did you remember something that you forgot?

Did you remember who you are?

Remember.

Write it down.

Tell someone.

Tell everyone.

🖁 Wake Up

Before you forgot, you had a plan. You knew where you were going and who you wanted to become. Because of negative thoughts along the way, much of that has not come true. Some of the dreams fell by the wayside in favor of newer, less inspiring ones. Born of a new situation created by events that were seemingly outside your direct control, you settled for the runner-up reality of making the best of a bad situation.

All you need to do now is wake up again, and remember who you are. It's all in there. All you really need to do is hold onto the possibility that things can get better than they have been. When you have such a possibility looming in your consciousness, when the doorway opens, you simply walk through it. You were just awaiting the opportunity to live it.

You must be
ready, willing and able
to receive the best-case scenario,

...and run with the ball...

An Amazing Life

You want to love your life. You must therefore awaken the part of yourself that still knows how to have a good time. Given the opportunity, people who have a positive outlook will engage in their chosen joyful activities whenever possible. Ultimately, positive choices are what lead to a happy life.

We get what we need when we choose to commit to doing what feels good to us. This is because once we feel good, we can continue this positive momentum into the specific acts that make up our lives. Ultimately, this is all that is necessary to sustain a profound sense of happiness throughout your life. If you are happy, everything seems to work out just fine.

It is a simple matter of like attracting like. If you are in a negative frame of mind, you can only attract and create negative things. If you continually strive to feel good in spite of adversity, you will find yourself with your head above water, no matter what the circumstances. In the end, you will find that the life experiences that you draw to you tend to feel good, in mirror image of your inner feeling.

Vibe matters.

The Magic of Appreciation

It is essential that we all allow ourselves to experience the relief of accepting things as they are. Everything is perfectly fine from the grand perspective. Noticing that this is the case is the only way to allow ourselves to experience absolute happiness, regardless of the current state of affairs.

That is not to suggest that you should embrace things as they are to the point of acceptance of what you do not like and forfeiting your dreams; Quite the contrary. It's just that you will never achieve everything you want to achieve because you will be continually inventing new dreams for yourself. In addition, your dreams are still in the making, and have not yet attained full expression. In the meantime, you must let things be as they are and allow yourself a sense of relief in your acceptance of where you are right now. From there, all good things will come. This feeling is the place from which we generate more abundance.

When you love where you are, you will be in the right mood to create your next steps. If you hate where you are, you will be magnetically connected to the feeling of your current state of affairs. This is merely a transitional stage if you allow it to be as it is, love the phase, and continually allow your mind to drift into better and better fantasies of what you want to create.

The feeling of acceptance and relief, more than any other emotion, is the one that allows you to get back in sync with what you want. If you are struggling, if you want something but can't seem to attain it, you are becoming addicted to the way of things as they are right now. You are becoming acclimatized to the state of not evolving, simply pacing in your cage.

The act of creation requires you to get into a feeling of satisfaction overflowing, abundance spilling over into a new manifestation of possibility. No other mood will allow you to create. No matter how hard you try, you cannot change things that are not to your liking, if all you do is complain about the current state of affairs. You must let things be as they are, relax into your life as it is, and then, from a place that is free of frustration, the change will come.

When you realize
that everything is perfect,
you will be free .

Specifics

In order to be a powerful creative force in your life, you must act now, in the present moment. This means getting down to specifics: figuring out exactly what it is that you want, realizing what needs to be done to make that happen, and actually doing it.

Successful, happy people operate in this way. They take the individual steps that lead them where they want to go. Furthermore, they surround themselves with people who love them enough to remind them of their dreams.

At various times in our lives, we are all given insight into what we want, and who we want to be. Occasionally, we share this dream with someone else. When this happens, we create something more sustainable than an unshared insight. This is because we now have someone else who sees what we see, which is exactly what begins the process of making a dream real. It becomes solid matter only after the complex chain of events caused by the receiver who first privately contemplates the epiphany, and then shares the concept with sincere, compelling enthusiasm.

This idea, whatever it is, is presented to the individual through his or her own inner wisdom and ability to see things as they are. It is pristine and perfect, with the original vibration of its untarnished essence still ringing in the head of the recipient. It has infinite potential and is as likely any thought in history to become realized in the world.

Depending on whether or not this idea is nurtured and evolved in the consciousness of the receiver, it may grow in clarity, or it may fade into the void. It will be gone until someone else realizes the same thing.

Fortunately, we do not need to have a "poverty mentality" about our ideas. Yes, it is a miracle every time a normal schmuck like you or me gets a big idea that could transform their world, or the world in general. It's just that ideas that are the absolute truth have a tendency to keep popping up every so often, all by themselves. That is simply because they are the truth. All you need to do is open your mind and let them in.

If you are willing to allow yourself the experience of utter amazement, you will find that you are capable of realizations of astonishing magnitude. Many of us have closed off our minds to such experiences for one reason or another. If, however, we awaken to the fact that we indeed want to embark upon such magnificent mental journeys, we will open ourselves to greater possibilities. We will allow ourselves to become a larger container of thought, and thereby become the great thinkers we were meant to be.

8 "Aha!"

The experience of epiphany is how you harness the ideas that bring about a life worth living. This is how the human being stands apart from the hustle and bustle of daily life, and transforms realized truth into physical matter.

Who you are is partly who you want to be, realized in moments of silence and joyful appreciation, and partly what you do in your moment-to-moment existence, as defined by your actions. Western culture is focused primarily on the action part. As many of us have realized, mere action is mostly impotent without inspired intent.

Discovering what it is that you want is the most important step in finding yourself in a place of real satisfaction with your life. Although intention is the beginning, without emotion there is nothing but an inert thought, elusive and fleeting. It can disappear if you do not allow yourself to get excited about it. It can be as if you had never had that thought at all...at least until you have it again.

If something is a higher truth for you, it will recur time and again, every time you sit down. It will be there in its perfect form, awaiting your open mind to come into view once again. It may, however, be a while before that happens. This is why you must act as soon as possible after the idea occurs to you.

You must stop and awaken, and then you must turn the potential into the kinetic by giving a form to your concept. You must write it down. Draw pictures around the words, with colored pencils or crayons. Make it more real by hanging the picture on the wall of your office. Infuse it with power by taking the time to light it up with energy.

Your idea is just another thought in your head until you give it more power. If you want to keep an insight alive, you have to invest yourself in it in every way. Make sure to remind yourself of your intention or idea every day. You must jog your own memory of the inspiration that you have experienced. No one else can do this for you.

Be creative about how you do this. Your positive emotion will help keep your dream alive in you. If you keep your dream alive, it will continue to evolve. Each time you think of it, the dream will become a bit clearer. As it becomes clearer, your negative thinking will have a harder time sinking its teeth into your vision. Eventually, the realization of your dream will become a certainty

If you can dream it, you can live it.

⚇ Put Your Life in Gear

We are all living in our own worlds. Each of us has either chosen or fallen into a reality that is intimately ours. Only you know how to walk your particular path. This means that the only person who knows exactly what is necessary to get things moving in your life is you.

What were you waiting for?

Do you have a book you haven't finished reading? Read it. Maybe there's something you need to say to someone but you haven't found the right opportunity to say it. You must say it. Maybe you're in a relationship that needs work. Choose to love them deeply, and without fear.

Whatever it is that you need to do, it's time to get off your lazy butt and do it.

Wellness and Laziness

When one views the actions of humanity as a whole, it is easy to conclude that we are a lazy species. We take such great pleasure in passive forms of entertainment, lounging in front of our TVs eating potato chips; it's a wonder how we ever mustered the energy to build a civilization in the first place. Such behavior, of course, is not what we truly want to be doing; it is just what we have fallen into due to habit and lack of creativity.

For many of us, we have found ourselves acting lazily due to what might be termed "cold fear". We have slipped into learned helplessness, unconsciously accepting that our failures of the past are likely to happen again and again. Consequently we give up and settle for boredom. We are simply too afraid to try.

In many cases, however, we act lazily simply because we are overworked, and don't rest and replenish ourselves as we should. Our skills of recuperation have become unacceptably inefficient, leaving us to look for rest at every possible opportunity. This means that we are never truly alive, even when we are in motion. We are not our fullest, brightest persona when we are exhausted, and we become incapable of making our dreams come true.

This is why we must take a holistic approach to living our lives. We must not ignore rest, nutrition, or joy. We must choose to relax fully, even if that means having a wild time first, wearing ourselves out, and then letting ourselves truly relax.

Sometimes up is down.

What are you about to do next, after you put down this book?

Do It Better.

Do it with your full attention.

By doing so, you will realize that these well-executed actions create a chain of events that create more positive possibilities. By paying attention to your life, chopping wood and carrying water, so to speak, you will find your whole life improving. By choosing to take steps to improve whatever is in front of you, everything improves, and you begin to activate your higher self.

Life progresses based on a far-reaching, meticulous gestalt that expands beyond our understanding, no matter how much knowledge and experience we have attained thus far. It is impossible to see all the inner workings of our success. From our perspective, first there is intention and inspired action, and then there is the world reflecting back to us with a mirror-like quality. Every aspect of your thoughts and actions reflect back to you in exquisite detail.

This is why your choice to act with a conscious, firm intention is the only way you can continue to operate from your higher self and the magnificent life that it creates. Your higher self wants you to pay attention to what you are doing, and have a fantastic life experience. Your lower self on the other hand, has a tendency to lose sight of this picture. You will frequently find your constricted, fear-based personality coming back to grab the steering wheel. This is when the moment of transcendence wakes you up to your higher intentions. You must let that version of you drive the bus.

This is the quantum jump from the lower personality, riddled with addiction and negative thinking, to the empowered personality that creates whatever it wants, and lives in the world of its own choosing. We have both voices in our heads, but only one needs to gain control over our thoughts and actions. We have a choice about what we do, and what we think.

Every day you must choose to switch yourself back on, to undertake to do the things you want to do and be the person you want to be. You must fully invest yourself in your actions, again and again, if you are to receive benefits on a harmonic frequency higher than that on which you have been living most of your life. This is the easy way to transform your life, since your higher self is and always will be the source of your creativity.

There is also a hard way. This is the path of arduous, uninspired effort. Action is almost always necessary, but if an action is not performed in the spirit of meaningful epiphany, it will not take us where we want to go. Worse, if the action is coupled with a sense of negative expectation, it can never lead us to the ultimate fruition of what we were originally trying to attain. The easy way, then, requires an attitude adjustment on the deepest level.

Your place of ultimate power to create is always your happiness. This is no surprise. Joy begets more joy; it comes in the form of all things beautiful and pleasurable. This is the purpose of creation in the first place. We create things that we wish to experience again, and if we're smart, we will manifest things that bring us happiness.

The realization of a particular aspiration that gives us a feeling of joy is, however, not the end. We must remain in touch with the original feeling of the dream, if we are to attain it in the most efficient way. Action is powerless to create when our inner feeling is not congruent with the feeling of our original intention. We must not lose sight of the dream because, ultimately, that is how we are bringing this thing into being.

This is the hard part. We have become so addicted to action that we have come to believe that action is how we attain. With our focus on action rather than on intention, we lose our connection to the feeling since we are engaged in the work part of the act of creation. We lose our sense that we have already attained it.

If you want to be in France, you need to picture yourself there. You also need to book a flight, but that is not really the hard part. The more challenging aspect is maintaining the belief that this possibility will become a reality. Our dreams often get swept aside by our pragmatic minds, or they are eroded by doubt, or fade with time. In order to be most effective in the process of creating, we must remember that the most significant aspect of the process is to hold onto the vision and feeling of your intention. Then you will discover that the action comes more easily, and there will be fewer stumbling blocks along the way.

Here is how it is done: First, connect with a meaningful vision for yourself. You know that it is a meaningful vision because you can feel it in your body whenever you think of it. It feels good to ponder this specific possible experience. Once this is done, your only real work is to release this desire into the world.

But here is the hard part. You must *actually believe* that this thing will come to pass. If you do not allow it to remain as a real possibility for you, you will get in the way of its coming into being.

To those fixated on the active part of life, this description appears incomplete. There must be *doing*, such people will say, in order to create. While this is often so, much less effort is required to get you where you want to go if the process is handled with clear intention preceding action, because the idea has been gestating, growing in possibility, on the non-physical plane of your consciousness. It has been busy making connections with other ideas that will help it to become reality.

It is true that the world operates in mechanistic ways, but the parts that are directly visible to the naked eye are just the tip of the iceberg. There are profound quantum effects of intention that can no longer be ignored.

Quantum physics suggests that things are just thoughts made concrete by belief and expectation. Believing that things can be different from the way they currently are is far more important than knowing and fixating on current conditions. If you want to be a powerful creator, you must understand that the way things are is not important. Envisioning things as you want them to be is the most important part of being the creator of your world.

*"Some men see things as they are
and say: Why?
I dream of things that never were
and say: Why not?"*

- George Bernard Shaw

Part Two

Who Are You?

Who Are You?

Who you are is ultimately a matter of choice. You may choose to continue living within the construct of your limited, fear-driven personality, but you know that that will just get you more of the same. I am suggesting you consider the possibility that you should decide that you are the kind of person who is going places in life. If you decide that this is true, it is far more likely to have it occur.

It is a simple matter of a decision, made in the now, to be the best version of yourself, to allow yourself to put everything you have into whatever it is what we are doing. That is the beginning of the creation of a realized being.

The path to an enlightened life is quintessentially mundane, as it is made over and over again in the simple moment-to-moment flow of your daily life. It is through the acts of eating, cleaning, working, and playing that you are given the opportunity to make real the original intention of your personal best-case scenario. Even a perfectly formed higher intention can be muddled and squandered by a lifestyle that limits the size of your container.

If you really consider who you are at your innermost core, you are simply positive intent. More specifically, you are a locus of perspective that desires experiences that lead to good feelings.

Even beyond that, you are an individual expression of a collective, universal desire for good feelings for all beings everywhere. In this, you and I and everything else, are one.

You Are Your Higher Self

You must choose to be your higher self. Why? Because it's better, that's why. You will be happier, plain and simple. Don't take my word for it; try it. You will discover, in no uncertain terms, that this is who you really are. All the other roles you have been playing are just products of your environment and of your neurosis. You do not need to own that, it is just where you have been. It is how you have learned what you are not.

If you would rather remain attached to your old ways of suffering, that's fine too. You learn what you need to learn just as easily by experiencing what you don't want as by experiencing what you enjoy. Inevitably, you will conclude that you want to be your higher self, and that you want your life to be a success.

Walk in your own shoes as well as you possibly can. By doing so, you will realize that what you do is important. It may not appear important right now, but it is important to somebody. The success of your life helps others to be happy, and inspires them to believe in the possibility of their having a better life.

You actually matter.

⑧ The Time Is Now

You know that you are constructing your world in the present moment. Your commitment to this very instant in time is what ultimately determines how your life will turn out. You must therefore choose to create your personal best-case scenario beginning right now.

This is a tall order. The commitment to the realization of the best-case scenario is the narrow path that becomes even narrower as you become more acutely aware of what it is that you want. The journey toward the perfection of human experience is fraught with danger on every level, requiring you to devote your full attention to the details of your surroundings. Fortunately, when you walk through the world with a clear intention, you significantly increase the likelihood of actualizing whatever you choose to create.

At times, you will be afraid. Fear will begin to hold you back. The closer you get to the realization of who you truly are, the more intense the resistance will be. Fear is like aerodynamic drag holding you back, and the faster you travel, the more drag tries to slow you down. Let the magnitude of your fear be your indication that you are getting closer to the life that is most powerful for you. You are tapping into the source of your energy.

Now that you are walking on the higher path, you must be careful in every way. The magnitude of the consequences to your actions increases when you decide to invest yourself in your best action. Inspiration comes with a cost. This means that you need to pay strict attention to your wellness on every level, because you cannot predict how much physical exertion you will need to carry out the next phase in life. Since you have already spoken your will that you will do your best, you must then make specific choices to improve your overall state of wellness, so that you are ready for anything.

This is the holistic approach to life: the unending, deliberately positive unfolding of reality though conscious action. You direct your experience toward a course of events that brings about what you ultimately want and need. This leads to a life that turns out to be more fun, and more nurturing of your spirit than you ever imagined.

Take Care of Yourself.

🎱 Overall State of Wellness

You must do your very best to be deeply healthy on every level. You cannot afford to allow your wellness to become degraded to the point that you lose power over your life, and thus make the near future more out of your control. Health is pivotal in your ability or inability to experience a positive future.

You must live your life to the fullest by creating health and well-being in every aspect of your life.

This is achieved on several fronts. A healthy individual is well nourished in every way. He or she is fit to the extent that they have the physical strength and energetic resources to stand up to anything likely to come their way. They invest themselves in a wide variety of activities that feed their souls, and they generally define themselves as deeply happy. They simply choose to allow themselves to engage in whatever activities and relationships bring them joy. They are complete human beings.

Who are these people? They are you and me, from time to time, whenever we make a series of choices that lead us to overwhelmingly positive

67

experiences. At such times, we allow things to go well because of the degree of our personal esteem. In short, we like ourselves, we like where we are, and everything flows from there.

If this were the worldwide state of affairs, there would be no reason to write or read books such as this. We fall. We live on the higher plane for a time, and then we screw up. Maybe all we do is allow ourselves to get physically and spiritually exhausted, and since we are not strong enough at the time, we fall short of a mark that matters. From this place of feeling bad, our thoughts about our potential to create begin to fade away, and we stop envisioning better possibilities. It is then, in the midst of our downward flow, that we must remind ourselves that everything is fine. When you realize this, it will begin to become true.

It is difficult to see the path laid out by our joy when we are on the trail of darkness. This is why it is important that we allow ourselves to indulge in what makes us happy. That way, when we find ourselves in that familiar place of anguish, we have to compare it to and something to connect with to bring us back to a place of. It is this contrast that helps us to discover and appreciate the things we love.

More importantly, we cultivate a connection to good feelings that we can tap into whenever we are preoccupied with thoughts and experiences that make us unhappy. If we dwell on what makes us feel lousy, we are powerless to dig ourselves out of the pit of despair. The light at the end of the tunnel recedes into the distance, and we begin to feel tired and helpless again.

Rather than carrying out our addiction to fixation on the negative side of things, we have the option of letting go of the feeling of despair by letting go of all thought, and then deliberately directing our minds back to something that makes us feel good again. From there we choose to eat good food, do yoga, and return to a feeling of balance and power. When we allow that to happen, the solutions eventually come to light. Even if there is no specific antidote to whatever is making us feel stuck, our change of perspective will begin to change how we feel about it, and in life in general. We are now moving forward again.

If we consider the possibility that all is well, and begin to see that things are exactly the way they need to be in order for us to learn whatever we need to learn at this moment, we will again tap into that sense of peaceful appreciation that connects us to the positive mood in which we are able to create. This mood gives us the ability to be happy again, which is ultimately the source of our creativity.

The mind expands when it is happy, and contracts when it is not. The feeling of happiness is not just a positive side effect of a good life; it is the reason for it. When we are feeling good, we are able to elaborate on what we love about life, and create more of whatever that is. We become empowered by the flow of energy that moves all life forward. When you are connected with this movement, you have the world on your side. Happiness is the fast moving center of the river. This is the source of all human energy.

When you dwell on what you do not like about your life, not only are you no longer able to expand and create what you yearn for, you are actually drawn toward that which you *do not* desire. The universe works in strange ways. If we are to become genuine innovators of the material world, we need to understand the powerful principle of the magnetic attraction of consciousness to its contents. Even modern science, in the field of quantum physics, has discovered and verified the validity of this concept. Matter is not what we once thought it to be. It is intimately connected to our state of mind.

If you try to justify why things are going badly and focus on how they are not to your liking, you are not part of the solution. You are simply drawing negative possibilities toward yourself, because you are not broadcasting anything other than what you are fixated on.

You must use your mind as it was meant to be used. If you desire something, hold on to that desire. Make it happen. If you do not want something, figure out how to avoid colliding with it, then let it go. Then all you need to do is consider what you *would* like to have instead.

The overall feeling of your mind is actually more important than any specifics that you may be conjuring. This is because the mind is only capable of creating more of what it is feeling. If you feel sad, you can only create sad thoughts; and therefore you only attract and create sad experiences. If you feel happy, you attract and create happy thoughts and experiences. No matter what confronts you, if you approach it in the most positive frame of mind possible, you will end up with a positive result.

The current state of affairs does not dictate everything that passes through your mind. You have the ability to maintain allegiance to the state of peace, happiness, love and anything else you define as good.

Switch It On

Surrender to being controlled by your
higher self,
the best version of you:

Meticulous
Clear
Attentive
Fascinated
Infatuated
Awakened
Appreciative
Joyful

Enlivened by purpose,
and the sheer thrill of being alive.

⑧ They May Call You Crazy

When you begin to tap into your creative self and start to work with higher levels of psychic energy, others will take notice. When we are in a place of sadness and hopelessness, people on a higher plane of happiness seem out of sync with what might be called reality. In truth, it is the joyful, creative people who are affecting reality to a greater extent.

Nevertheless, those who are feeling disconnected from their inner creative nature will continue to condemn those who are going with the flow of joy.

You do not need to change the attitudes of those around you. In the end, your success and happiness are all the influence needed to change the world for the better. If you require everyone around you to see things your way, you will find yourself fighting a losing battle. You may even discover that your vibration begins to slow to their level, and you begin to feel unhappy. This is because you are not allowing them to be as they are.

All beings are on their own trip. Your journey, your vision, and your happiness—these things are entirely up to you. You can never allow the experience of others to dull your vibe. Let them call you crazy. Let them mock your ways, if that is what they need to do in order to affirm their own reality. They will find sanity in their own way. Your job is to maintain your own happiness, in your personal way. Allow them to be who they are, and you will have an easier time being who you are.

When one achieves a moment of enlightenment, it is easy to believe that you are the only one who has experienced this. By feeling alone in having your vision, you begin to think that, unless you convince others to see things as you do, you will lose connection to your vision. Nothing could be further from the truth.

All beings are capable of enlightenment. When you realize this, you will not try to convert others to seeing things the way you do. Their path up the mountain is based on their own personal journey, and it will not be the same as yours. You have to trust that their path is perfect for them, and honor the fact that they may have already gotten to the place where you are. When you honor their wisdom and their journey, you will find that they begin to honor yours.

I'm OK.
You're OK.

There is a Difference

between girls and women,
boys and men,
ordinary and exceptional,
cowardly and brave.

If you realize what you truly stand for
and continually strive toward this end,
willing to forgive yourself
your occasional shortcomings along the way,

... you will continue to expand.

If you maintain your allegiance to this goal,
you will continue the process
of creating your Higher You.

🎱 You Are Your Focus

Every moment of every day, by dwelling on some thoughts and dismissing others you are selecting the thoughts that will determine who you become. You can evolve into who you really are, or you can become an expression of who you are not. One path leads to a positive future; the other doesn't.

When we focus our energy on the things that do not feel good to us, we feel friction in the form of emotions like fear, anger, and sadness. This happens in order to create a clearer picture of our intentions for who we want to be with the expression of our living persona. In this way, negative emotion can help us to connect with who we really are, like an internal compass.

You are who you are; you always have been. This is not meant in a limiting way at all. Your ideals, attractions and aversions ultimately define who you are. But you have not always acted in harmony with these truths. You have spent a great deal of your time dodging the responsibility of being this person by allowing the ideas of others to determine your self-image. You have allowed your negative thoughts to dictate your actions.

These thoughts are much more than just flashes in the pan of your mind. If you hold on to them, they are the shape of things to come. The thoughts that you repeat over and over in your mind eventually manifest themselves physically, while the ones that you think once and then let go of, tend not to turn into material experiences.

You can only change the progress of your life by altering *what* your mind is focused on, by choosing to dwell only on creative ideations. Thoughts entertained on a regular basis are the ones that manifest into reality, simply because they attract the specific things that will allow them to come into being.

If you have ever tried to create something, you will recall the emotional release you felt at the first occurrence of your idea. You must be in the space of this feeling as you progress through the evolutionary process that brings it into being. If you focus on the reasons why your dream cannot become a reality, you will attract exactly the kind of negative energy that will prevent it from becoming.

You must resonate on the frequency of your dream. The thought-form of your invention is purely your own, and the only one who knows what it feels like is you. You may inspire others to actualize it but, in the end, if you lose your connection to the original feeling, you will be flying your dream remotely, rather than being in the pilot's seat of the vehicle of your creation.

What does the life you want to live feel like? It is this sensation that will allow you to make it occur in physical form. This feeling is the source of your power. Beyond words, beyond ideals, beyond morals, there is vibration; there is feeling. Nothing matters more than your happiness. Nothing empowers you more as a creator. This is how you connect with who you are and tap into your unlimited creative power. You must close the gap between who you are on the outside and who you are on the inside.

Who are you?

Better than you originally imagined.

Way better.

Mood and Thought

We all have emotional thoughts that help guide us through life. Not all emotions, however, are beneficial for the process of creating what we want to create. Some are simply warnings about things that we think may harm us in some way. We need these feelings, but we do not always need to elaborate on the content of our minds when we are in such a feeling-state.

A more productive way to handle feelings is to understand what they are telling us, and then bring ourselves to a place of positive emotion before we create a specific course of action. When we view our lives from this place, things look completely different. In fact, things happen differently too.

The person you most want to be resides in your place of feeling good. This is where you connect with your inner essence. This is where you use your emotions to fuel your dreams for yourself and the world. You tap into a limitless resource of information by being in the same feeling-place as the information. If you feel wonderful, if you appreciate your life, you are open to the flow of self-knowledge that originates in that place of happiness and abundance.

All too often we strive for positive thoughts and changes from a place of feeling bad. This is never the way out of where we are. In order to generate positive thoughts that create solutions, we must first allow ourselves to think thoughts that make us happy. This may involve actually doing things that bring you joy, like playing with children, or simply conjuring the feeling by revisiting the experience in your mind. There really is no difference, since the result is the same. When you begin to feel good again, you can do just about anything.

From the perspective of your powers of creativity and your ability to generate change, there is nothing more important than how you feel. The only way to bring about things that reflect your higher self is to be your higher self. Do whatever you need to do to bring yourself to that place of feeling good, so that you remain in connection to who you really are—intensely happy, appreciative, and hopeful about the future.

Anger is Information

When you are angry, it is possible that you are simply tired and cranky. That is your indication that you need to get back to the ongoing job of taking care of yourself. If, however, your anger is coming from a specific situation that requires action, you must remain in balance and do whatever needs doing.

Let your anger speak to you. Notice the feeling, take a long, slow breath to get your body back under control, and ask yourself exactly *what* you are angry about. When you understand what you dislike in your reality, send your thoughts in the direction of the best possible version of this situation for everyone concerned; including you.

When you use the wisdom of your emotions, you can tap into your knowledgeable inner voice. There is no better teacher than the core of who you are and what you know to be good and right. As you commit your efforts to realizing this goal, your idea of a "higher good" continues to evolve. Slowly you expand your sense of self, and consequently you will be given more power to create change in the world.

Do not push your emotion away. Say thank you to it. Although you may not choose to act on all the thoughts that came into your head while you were under the influence of the emotion, if you deliberately listen, you can glean profound teachings about what you want to do. Then all you need do is take deliberate, positive, constructive action.

You are the creator of your personal world.

Start acting like it.

⦾ Limitations

If you are unhappy, your true essence is not the problem; it never was. You are an unlimited being, motivated by the most beautiful dreams for yourself and the people around you. If you are unhappy, it is because you have not been actualizing these possibilities; you have been living in a second-best version of your world, which you did not plan to live in when you originally conceived your life.

As your life progresses down the timeline of possibility and choice, you have altered the direction and embodiment of your experience. You have become something different from what you originally intended. In some ways, this embodiment is better, and in some ways, it is worse. If your choices and ideas are based on fear and the belief that you are a fundamentally limited, your reality will become sadder and more helpless.

You are not limited. You never were. Your thoughts, however, tend to recur. Restrictive thoughts recur because of your fear, habits, and laziness; they therefore become your experience. You are limited not because of who you are, but because of what you think. You allow these habitual, limiting thoughts to recur in your head, in the belief that they reflect your deeper reality. In truth, these thoughts are nothing less than the cause of it.

You are what you think.

Creation begins and ends with thought. Depending on how often you think a thought and how much you magnify the expression of its original feeling, you will either develop it into something much larger and more complex, or allow it to fade away. You have allowed some of your most beautiful dreams to dissipate into the ether of your consciousness, because you have focused your mind on whatever was right in front of you, and you let this original idea disappear. This is how your life turns into something you believe you did not choose.

The present moment requires your full attention, but not to the extent that you forget where you are going. Who you are must not be absorbed into what is happening right now. Can you imagine what it would be like if, while driving, you forgot your name whenever you paid attention to the road in front of you? We are more complex than that. We have the ability to pay complete attention to our surroundings, while remaining aware of who we are, and where we are headed in life.

It is the loss of this ability that has allowed many of us to fall into what appear to be miserable lives not of our choosing. We have, of course, chosen every aspect of our experience, though not always as the result of our conscious decisions. We look at our present reality and see that it does not harmonize with our original intent; so we decide that we did not make things as they are. If we were completely in control of our reality, things would be exactly as we had originally wanted them to be, wouldn't they?

Wrong. We create our moment-to-moment experience within the space of our thinking. Many of us believe that our thoughts are not subject to our control. We believe that we are victims of our thinking, and victims of our reality. Neither of these is true.

Furthermore, we allow ourselves to dwell on visualizations of the negative in an effort to prevent it from happening; but this effort only results in the manifestation of more of what we do not want. The universe does not understand the word "No." It hears what we think, and magnetizes more of what we hold in our minds. It is entirely up to the thinker to decide what value judgment to pass on what is focused upon.

If you do not like the content of your mind, you must not dwell on it. This is how you create exactly what you do not want. If you want to avoid a negative experience, you must visualize a positive one in its place. This is how the mind works, and trying to use it in any other fashion will result in failure.

If you want to create something,
envision it as clearly as possible.

If you want to destroy something,
envision creating something else in its
place.

There is no such thing as
"No"

There is only
"Yes"
to something else.

Being Happy

When you awaken to the thoughts and experiences that make you whole, you will notice that which makes you profoundly happy. When you do these things, you are being who you are.

You may have viewed this part of your experience as positive reinforcement—the reward for the sacrifices you have made in the past. If you work in order to feel joy, you will always be living short of your full potential. Allow your joy to become your life.

"Follow your bliss."
-Joseph Campbell

When you are steeped in your joy, you are unstoppable. This is not a feeling that you should reserve for occasional perfection. This is where you must reside. If you live in joy, everything comes to you the way you want it. This is so because the kinds of thoughts that occur to you when you are happy will lead you to more of the same: Like attracts like.

Your life can only be perfect when you begin to realize that it already is perfect. Yes, there are things to change to make life easier and even more enjoyable, but these changes cannot take place until you begin to tap into the limitless resources of happiness.

Did you think that you were going to find your way to happiness by toiling and complaining? That is just a waste of time and energy. If you want to create something, you must live in the feeling of that which you want to experience. Holding your feeling elsewhere will only bring you somewhere else.

We often find ourselves waiting until we attain certain goals before we give ourselves permission to be happy. Perhaps you think you need a certain academic degree or a certain dollar amount in your bank account. Perhaps you believe that you need someone special in order to feel complete. Although these things will give you a concrete reason to give yourself permission to acknowledge yourself and be happy, satisfaction is not guaranteed even when you have all achieved all that you thought was necessary. That permission still remains entirely up to you.

If your self-permission to be happy is based solely on external conditions, you will not be able to sustain this feeling, nor conjure it when you most need it. You will always strive to live up to higher expectations for greater achievements before you give yourself full permission to love yourself; because once you attain these conditions, you will realize that you are still basically the same person, with all of the same old neurotic, negative patterns of thought. You take your self-doubt with you wherever you go.

This is why your decision to greenlight your existence cannot be conditional. You must decide that you are already in a state of perfection, and that these validating actions are merely your ways of demonstrating who you really are. Only then can you reach a sustainable condition of happiness and fulfillment.

You must do the things that show the world who you are. You must start with a personal connection to who you are and what you believe, so you can express it to the world. Otherwise, you will be striving to do things in order to be who you are, in the mistaken belief that you must earn your self-love. If you want to take the long path to self-fulfillment, by all means try to attain a higher goal while holding in your heart a sense of inadequacy. Let me save you the trouble: this will not work.

The conditions in your life that are bringing you down are merely signs of the current status of your journey. They merely indicate where you are right now. From a certain standpoint, who you have been, who you are now, and who you are becoming all exist in the same space, and seeing your life from this place is the only way to transcend the suffering that is created by comparing where you are now to where you are going.

When you are mentally stuck on who you are right now, you are inadvertently working to maintain the present state of affairs. If, instead, you visualize what would be the result of your most positive thinking, you will begin to see the specific steps you need to take in order to get there. You will be able to picture what it would be like to be that person, and in doing so you will be able to make it so.

You must decide what you want to do and commit to doing it. This may seem impossible from your present standpoint, but if you believe that you are able to do it, it immediately begins to take shape. If you cling to the way things have been, in an effort to prevent yourself from forgetting what you do *not* want, you will generate a magnetic force that drives you toward this negative outcome. You must continually refresh your connection with the feeling, nature, and specifics of your dream in order to make it come true.

If you do not, you will find yourself living an uninspired life. You will be wasting your limited time on this planet hiding in the shadows of mediocrity. Like the bud of a flower that has not yet blossomed, your true nature will remain hidden from the world.

Worrying that you will be unable to achieve your goals will not help you achieve them.

You must put an end to all thoughts that do not tell you where you want to go and how you are going to get there. When such corrosive thoughts return—and they will—greet them the way you would greet an old friend who no longer reflects the way of your new life. Give them your complete love and your complete forgiveness, and release them back into the wild. You may then return to the job of making your dreams come true.

*Thinking too hard
is the root of all incompetence.*

Let life flow.

Let your love of your world
shine through you.

All things flow from love:
Love of what you are doing,
Love of the people around you,
Love of the earth beneath your feet,
and the sky beneath your wings,
Love of it all.

Invest yourself in life.

Life progresses based
on the authenticity of the effort.

Believe in what you are doing,
and you will succeed...

...often with Flying Colors.

There is an ultimate version of you, floating around in Infinite Possibility.

Allow it to become.

If you are having fun,
Keep doing it.

Whatever it is...

It's good for you.

You are allowed to be happy.

Dare to believe in what you are doing.
Let yourself try to do it better.

Whatever it is,
it is bound to lead to more success.

No matter how small, success in creating an experience that you wanted to create will generate momentum. It will continue the process of turning you into a realized being. It will take you one step further along the way to being convinced that you are who you thought you were.

You are the source
of your experience.

Part Three

Your Personal Journey

⦂ The Right Direction

Why haven't you succeeded in every aspect of your life? Because you haven't committed all your resources to getting what you want. When you fail to invest your whole self in action, often it is because you have chosen a goal that is not good for you, or not good for the people around you. You may know this on an unconscious level, and this fact may be robbing you of motivation. Or maybe you really are being held back by the world, because you have chosen an idea whose time has not yet come, maybe never will come.

You must always consider the possibility that what you are doing with your life is not the right direction for you. If it is not, you will be powerless to create on a higher level, and this makes it will harder for you to achieve true happiness in your life.

How do you know if you are on the right path? Ask yourself the following question:

> *How do I feel when I think about*
> *the person that I have become?*

To get a more specific answer, you must examine yourself from two different perspectives:

The first relates to who you believe you are compared with who you are acting like; the role that you are playing in life. If you discover that your role is at odds with the image of your true inner self, you must find a way out of this predicament.

You must be who you are.

This may require modifying your outlook so as to infuse your present lifestyle with meaning and joy. It may require a more radical change in your life. But, either way, it is imperative that you make the necessary changes when you realize the incongruity between image and reality. If you suppress your inner being, you will effectively cut off your own life force and deprive the world of your personal gifts. If you don't play the part of being you, no one is going to do it for you.

The second way in which to examine yourself requires you to examine how your life's work fits in with your own concept of what constitutes meaningful change in the world. This has a very different definition for each of us.

The truth is, there are many different answers to this question, and all are important. We need to collectively explore and cultivate the millions of possible answers to this question if we wish to keep this planet afloat and our species physically healthy, mentally balanced, and deeply happy.

Some of you will feed the hungry.
Some of you will build shelter for the homeless.
Some of you will heal the sick and injured.
Some of you will be inspiring teachers.

We need you all.

Please do your thing.

There are many meaningful paths,
and they are all holy.

Give your particular gifts to the world.

Let it shine.

We Need You

We need your unique perspective; your individual experiences and epiphanies. You matter to the universe. Your purpose is to explore your reality, discover what you truly stand for and enjoy, and do it. If you walk this kind of path, you will begin to create a brand-new branch of existence, which widens the universal perspective by one more exquisitely specific set of realized possibilities and truths. This is how you give back to the universe.

The trick is to keep being what you love about yourself. Have a good time. Let yourself be happy. This is how you find your way. If it does not feel good, it's not what you want to be doing. Learn from your experiences, both positive and negative, complete whatever it is that life is requiring you to do, and then move on; back to the person you love being.

Do you get to be the person you want to be, day in and day out? This must be your goal, as you look ever deeper into what you truly believe and what brings you the greatest joy. You will find these things not by thinking, but by feeling. If you just sit down and clear your head, your gut will tell you what to do.

Your body will guide you. If you notice the way that energy flows through your physical body, you will clearly know whether what you are doing or thinking is a source of truth and power. This energy speaks to you in the language of physiology, stoking the fire of your limbic system, and it will generate thoughts that may or may not go in the direction in which you ultimately want to go.

The thoughts and actions that occur to you when you are in the initial, intoxicating phase of an emotional experience are often detrimental to the central, sane goal that stirred up the emotion in the first place. At some time or other, we have all acted out of passion, and discovered that sometimes passion can lead us astray. A wise person realizes that he or she must examine the appropriateness and constructiveness of thoughts before they are turned into action.

When we consider the meaning of the emotion and how to channel our thoughts in a beneficial direction, there is a shift in possibilities. You now have the potential to create a set of realistically achievable experiences that you find more desirable than those suggested by your primary charge of emotion. Instead of finding yourself responding in a stereotypical way to a given emotion, you can use the emotion as your guide to discover what it is that you ultimately wanted to do. This allows you to use the power of the emotion, but still control it and put it to good use.

When you realize who you are,
there is nothing left to do
but do it.

*Resume being
the best version of you.*

Where Are You Going?

Is it where you originally wanted to go?

Are you living an outdated dream that you created in an earlier chapter of your life?

It is possible that where you are currently headed is the wrong place for you, or for the world around you.

If this is so, get on it.
Make the change.

Do not let fear stop you.
Do not let laziness stop you.

Never settle for unhappiness.

Once you know what makes you happy,

you absolutely *must* do it.

⦚ Are You on Your Path?

Remember who you are when you are happiest, and be that person. When you are being that person, things will be as they should be in your life. You may not make a million dollars. You may not walk on the moon. That doesn't matter. If you are being who you really are, you are on the right track.

If you can smile about your life, you are on one of the right paths. If you feel sad when you consider your path, you need to make changes. Do not lament your errors. Just do what you need to do to get yourself back to happiness.

Eventually, you will feel better when you ask these kinds of questions. Not at first, maybe. You are bound to have growing pains. In the end, you will come to know yourself and your ideals and you will see that, although you may not yet fully express who you know you are, at least you are on your way to making it happen.

*You will never
complete the process
of becoming who you are.*

*Your character
is not yet fully revealed,
because you are still in the
process of inventing
You.*

And that is perfect too.

⦿ Prosperity

If you thought that greenlighting your life meant finding a formula to get rich quick—sorry, it doesn't always work that way. Some of you are karmically ready to get rich; some of you are not. Some will use your powers of manifestation to acquire money, but due to lessons that you need to learn, you will lose that wealth. Some of you will become incredibly powerful creators, but will choose to focus your influence on matters of compassion and generosity instead.

How this plays out is a matter of your long-term journey. It may not turn out as what you now envision as success, but it is still going to be a perfect way for you to reach your own enlightenment. The human spirit has the ability to find a way to let light shine in no matter how painful the circumstances. Many of us have found, in fact, that adversity actually brings out the part of us that we were always hoping was there.

When Hurricane Katrina hit, everyone was affected. Whether we were in the floods or watching it on TV, we all knew what was happening. We were all in it together. One man watched his TV in Texas and saw an animal hospital with hungry animals that weren't being fed. He owned a helicopter. He went out, bought pet food, got in his helicopter, and flew the food to the hospital that he had seen on TV.

Becoming a great person is not a matter of money. It is true that financial power gives us the ability to create certain kinds of changes in the world. For those of you who are ready to take on the responsibility of wealth, do it in style. Do it with grace. Do it with meaning. If you use your wealth to become just another consumer, filling your coffers with useless crap and meaningless experiences, it will not make you a better person. It will take you further from the person that you ultimately wanted to be.

The actions that make us proud to walk our own path define us and show us our fundamental nature. Unfortunately, we do not always breach our fear and lethargy in order to act in such a manner, but we know we want to. We just chicken out. This is why the world is in such a state of need.

It doesn't matter *how* you are helping others; what matters is that you *are* helping. This is how real energy is collected. Even if you do not make money from the benevolent choices you make, you will get what you need. The cook is always fed.

Ultimately,
all we ever really need
is to believe in what we are doing
and appreciate what we have.

That is real success.

No amount of money can buy that.

🎰 Happy Vibes

If you are having fun, you are in your place of highest vibration. This is where you are most creative, and most powerful. Let this feeling spread from one deliberate act to the next. Let your choices be based on your bliss and the voice of your inner being. This is the hallmark of an empowered life, one that puts you in a place of conscious creation.

Do and think what makes you vibrate at a higher frequency. This vibration is what gives you the ability to invent better possibilities, because you are in touch with the higher you. When you are truly feeling good, you will be in connection with your inner sage and all of its wisdom.

The more often we think a thought, the more real it feels to us, and the less we investigate the fundamental truth of it. We often find ourselves by sheer inertia carrying on with an idea that was created in the climate of a lower vibrational frequency. Then we find ourselves creating more things that feel like that, even if that is not what we desire. The creative forces of the universe are based more on the frequency and duration of a persistent thought than on the degree to which we truly believe in this thought.

This is a very important idea. When we dedicate our time and energy to ideas that we do not want anymore, we find ourselves living the life of someone we were in the past, rather than being a present reflection of our inner nature.

Remember, you are expanding. You are growing into a more purpose-filled life. If you want to see your inner self to have an effect on the physical world, you must continually adjust your thinking and update the version of who you are. You must let go of thoughts that do not take you where you want to go, and you must not look back. The inertia of who you have been will persist into the future, but you cannot allow this to alarm you or cause you to become self-aggressive. You cannot beat yourself up for having a persistent attraction to something that you have repeatedly asked for in the past.

Your present is an average of your past and present thoughts and action "requests." Do not let it bother you that you are not always the perfect expression of your highest self. You are at all times in a state of improvement, and this means that you have to constantly resynchronize your outer being with your inner being. This is the journey of life, as your character unfolds toward its full expression.

⦚ Being Well

Your vision of your future must include all aspects of the balance that constitutes a good life. You must be "well" on every level of your being in order to be a genuinely successful person. True wellness includes body, mind, and spirit.

This requires you to ground your energy in silence, which is a state that is much more difficult to achieve in a state of need. When your body is unfulfilled on a physical level, you are not a large enough vessel capable of holding your highest vision of you.

Repeatedly choose to remember
to take care of yourself in every possible way:

Nurture your body.

Nurture your mind.

Nurture your spirit.

Drink more water.

Eat healthy food.

Take care of your teeth.

*Keep your body
strong and flexible.*

Indulge yourself
in the wide variety of activities
that make you whole.

*Clear your head
whenever you can.*

*Slow down
when you are going too fast.*

Figure out what makes you happy.

Do it.

⦚ Surrounded by Goodness

The pace of life is so fast today that we all have to be selective about what to include in our day. We can fill our heads with mindless drivel, or we can feast on inspiring information that reminds us who we are.

You must surround yourself with things that help point you in the direction of the real you. Collect music, books, movies, and other experiences that bring back your feeling of true happiness and fascination with the world. Hang post-it notes with your highest insights, and put them in places that you will frequently pass in your daily life. If you encircle yourself with positive meaning, you will magnetically attract more of the same.

Love everything that makes you feel good. Choose to do what you love doing, and indulge yourself in that love by allowing yourself to actually enjoy it. Surrender to the life that happiness invites you to live. Alternative possibilities will simply not be as much fun or as gratifying, not matter how hard you try.

Immerse yourself in experiences that bring out your higher self.

⧉ Levels of Truth

Just as macroscopic particles are subject to physical laws and their behavior is thus largely predictable, so human behavior on a mass scale is mostly predictable. This, of course, is not the essence of who we are on an individual level. It may be where we came from, but it is not the source of our brilliance.

Just as quantum mechanics shows that the behavior of individual particles at the subatomic level is completely unpredictable, so human behavior on the individual level is unpredictable. This unpredictability is the fundamental nature of the life force that makes us beautiful. We are independent beings with an infinite capacity for novel points of view and lively inspirations that expand what is possible.

That is why you are here: not just to observe what already exists, but also to add to it, develop it, and make it your own. The real magic of consciousness is what happens in the moment, on an individual level. You are awake, and your perspective is novel. This is how the universe grows in complexity. This is the purpose of individual consciousness.

The Universe is glad that you are here.

⁞ Expand

You matter more when you open yourself to the possibility of unhindered creativity and expansion. Let yourself become. Let yourself radiate. Question everything around you, and find ways to make more out of what is right in front of you. In this way, you will be answering the greatest cosmic question of all: "What more is there?" The answer to this question is the very reason for the universe.

You must derive your forward movement from the answer to this question, so that the answer helps you discover more of who and what you are. Greenlighting your existence is simply a matter of connecting with your own creative inner nature that stems from your true self. Holding still in fear is not an expression of who you are; it's just a trap that you occasionally fall into. It is not wrong, it just shows you where the path is not.

The mind is not expanded by confining your attention to what is. Anyone can observe reality and accept it in its current state. Expansion results from inquiry and a commitment to the ongoing process of finding the answers that make things better. You must ask the questions that help you to define who you are:

*Who am I
when I am being my highest self?*

What does my highest self
want me to do
right now?

What actions, roles and situations help me to feel like my true self?

What does happiness mean to me?

*What brings light into the world
in my own personal color?*

What can I do to make my world
a better place?

*What will bring me into
alignment
with who I am
at my innermost core?*

What deeply inspires me?

How can I enliven my existence with purpose?

What has been holding me back?

Is it a relationship that needs healing?

*Am I continuing to pay
an emotional debt
that has already been settled?*

*Am I holding onto a persistent
belief about myself
that is limiting
and therefore not true?*

Have I forgotten something about who I am?

Have I forgotten that I am already living an incredible life?

Have I forgotten that I am really good at what I love to do?

*Do I believe that I do not deserve
to live on a higher plane of
happiness?*

*Did I realize something profound,
but then simply forgot it
when I returned to the routine
of my daily existence?*

If something like this is gnawing at you—most likely, there are many such things—you absolutely must take care of business, whatever that means to you. You cannot greenlight your life until you do.

Write it down, and do it.

Keep the Fire Burning

If you are to continue to be an inspired person, you must repeatedly ask the following question:

"Where can I find knowledge that will light the fire of my being?"

If you surround yourself with mundane thoughts and experiences, you will just magnetize more of them same, and you will find yourself feeling uninspired and unhappy. If, on the other hand, you take deliberate action to surround yourself with people, experiences, and ideas that wake you up and fill you with zest for life, you will attract exactly that kind of experience.

Go to the theater and see an inspiring play. Go see a movie that makes you think. Read books that challenge you to ponder how to make your life more fun, exciting, and liberating. Listen to speakers whose passion ignites your vision, and sets your spirit free to be who you want to be. What you do becomes what you are.

🎰 Using Your Power

We can break through the strong forces of inertia using the power of emotions like anger, hatred, frustration, and rage. There are things to hate in this world, and in your life. By working with your authentic emotions brought to you through your real life experiences, you can get your boat to run downwind, and away from where you are: stuck in a place you don't want to be. Use the power to realize what you do not love, and choose to direct your life toward experiences that bring you happiness.

The trouble is, you cannot see joy from a place of misery. You are so far away from positive experience when you are suffering that you cannot relate to happiness at all. You must work with the experience of what you are living right now; even it is not in itself joyful at first glance. From a certain perspective, your life, whatever it is, is far better than it could be. This is the perspective of appreciation, where the light comes in.

Despair is the ultimate enemy. It is the frozen place where be begin to think that we cannot change things for the better. Powerful emotion presents the potential for change. It is movement and, ultimately, that is how we progress beyond the place of inaction and helplessness. Once the movement begins, the energy can be transformed into the vision of things getting better.

Here is how you make the transition from frozen hopelessness into flowing happiness:

You transform your *hopelessness* into *anger* about the aspect of the situation that you hate.

Transform your *anger* into *desire for retribution* so that the situation will return to a state of balance.

Then you can transform your *desire for retribution* into the *hope* of something better when the situation is resolved.

Transform your *hope* into the *belief* that this will actually happen.

Transform your *belief* into *action* by being your highest, happiest self in this specific context.

The high state and the low state do not touch directly. They require a process of flowing metamorphosis in order to progress from one into the other. Trying to work things any other way is how you fall into the learned helplessness that keeps you feeling stuck. Allow your emotions to divulge their true meaning, and you will be able to satisfy the urge that the emotion is asking you to satisfy. You can then return to creating a wonderful life.

We all have an aversion to unpleasant emotions. This is only natural, because we do not enjoy the experience of contraction. We strive to remain in good feelings, but in doing so we often miss the chance to access the true joy of riding the wave of our authentic experience. If you confront whatever your negative emotion is asking you to resolve, you will be able to rejoin the party at a much higher level.

Emotion is a river that only flows one way. It flows forward. Its course may be chaotic at times, but ultimately it is headed where you want to go. Getting out of the river will not get you where you want to go, but neither will paddling against the current. Turn your boat the current of the river of your experience, and go with the flow. This is where life wants you to go. Anything else will cause you unnecessary suffering and hardship.

If life feels difficult and hopeless, it is because you are going against the current. You are working against the energy. The energy comes from the truth of how you really feel. The power of your inner knowing speaks to you through your fear and your joy, and carries with it information about which is the easy way to go, and which is the hard way.

You are better at things you enjoy doing. You are good at them because you love to do them. You allow yourself to focus on what you are doing because of the intrinsic motivational value of the experience. You simply like how you feel when you do it.

This is why 'going with the flow' works better than the alternative. If you are not totally invested in what you are doing, totally digging it, you will not be able to truly shine. Too often we find ourselves adopting a "fake it 'til you make it" attitude. We cannot allow ourselves to do that with our dreams. Inauthenticity has tragic consequences.

Your emotions are the beginning of your next step upward. This will always be so, because no matter how hard you focus on whatever it is you are doing, something will always be nagging at you, telling you how you really feel. If you ignore that nagging just because it is breaking your concentration and "ruining your buzz," you will be ignoring the wisdom of your inner being. Your actions will be incongruent with how you really feel.

Worse, if you do not pay heed to what your emotions are telling you about what you want and don't want, you disconnect yourself from the power of the situation that can propel you forward into the next experience in your life with more positive energy. If you act in alignment with who you are, you will always be in your element.

Each emotional reaction you have is information that something requires your attention. That need is like weight in the basket of the hot air balloon of your psyche. When you satisfy its essential need, you shed weight. You shed the heaviness of your bad feelings, and you are allowed to be happy again. In the end, isn't that what life is all about?

Set your spirit free.

⦂ Higher Stakes

Fear increases with risk. The more dangerous your situation, the more powerfully your fears will work in opposition to your direction of motion.

When you are in physical danger, the end result of things going badly is obvious and irrefutable. This indirectly results in the physiological changes in your body that gear you up to act with huge power. This results in new physical possibilities that did not exist in your normal state of consciousness.

Truly being yourself, and indulging in what resonates with you on the deepest level, can trigger an even more intense reaction of fear and resistance. When this kind of intense reaction takes place, it is essential for your well-being that you not run away from the source of your fear. You may even choose to proceed with caution, once you understand the rules of the situation and how to manage its risks.

You must choose to confront the things that scare you most if you are to discover who you are. Further, you must take emotional risks, so that you can connect with your most powerful energy of all. This is how you work on the highest plane of insight and inspiration. It begins as a choice to snap out of your bad trip, the fear and the resistance, and allow yourself to do the things that wake you up. You must do these things partly because doing them keeps your life energy young and vital, but also for the sake of what you will learn from confronting your most powerful enemy, your fear-driven thought processes.

When we give in to fear, we are not trying to resolve whatever provoked the fear in the first place. That can only be done from a positive frame of mind. Even in the face of real danger, we must always greet fear with a smile. Fear can only be dissolved by Love. Love the moment for what it is. Let it be, and accept it completely. This is how you will connect with the essential inner cool that relaxes the fear and transforms it into focus; the kind of focus that leads us to joy; the kind of joy that makes dreams come true.

*When you realize that there is no fear
that cannot be dissolved by love,*

*you will begin to shed your fear
of being afraid.*

Part Four

Awakening Your Higher Self

⧅ Clear Out Your Mind

Something happens when you clear your mind. You stop being your separate self, your ego, and begin connecting with the part of you that is connected with everything else. When this happens, nothing stands between you and infinite wisdom; nothing prevents you from opening your mind to any possibility, no matter how grand.

You must exercise this skill as you would exercise a muscle. When the mind is allowed to drift back into its unruly habits of behavior, you lose your ability to choose your focus. It is your ability to focus that allows you to understand anything, do anything, and become anything.

Focused attention is not our natural state. The mind wants to pay attention to everything at once, so as not to miss out on anything. This kind of consciousness is not clear and complete in its attention to any one aspect of our reality, because instead of listening to one thing at a time, it is listening to everything at once.

Try to focus your mind. Go deeper into something in your field of awareness, a tree, a sound, a breath. Let your mind remain connected to this thing so profoundly that there is nothing else. Keep this sharp focus for a bit longer. Let go of distractions. Let the alternative objects of your attention drift away, while you keep your mind on what you are paying attention to at that moment.

You will become aware of many things as you do this. Some your mind will present as more important. Alternative objects of your attention will always come up. Do not expect that they will fade away as you "get good at" paying attention. Yes, your relationship to distraction will change as you practice maintaining focus, but you will never maintain complete and singular focus forever. In fact, that is not the goal of meditation at all. The goal is to remain in the present moment, whatever it is; to be here now.

It is true that there are things in the "distraction field" that are important. It is true that sometimes these "distractions" become salient enough that they require immediate action. Most often, however, we use that possibility as an excuse to chase every "rabbit" that comes into our awareness. This is how we remain unfocused beings, unable to realize our will in the world.

When there is nothing in your reality but your object of attention, focusing on it is effortless. It is always easier to meditate in a cave. It is good to take yourself out of the torrent of life and simplify your situation. In these times you can permit yourself to focus deeper on the object of your attention, and into your experience of feeling good. You can allow yourself to indulge your awareness of the moment, and surrender to investing your complete, undivided attention. By allowing yourself to collect mental resources in the present moment, you connect with the part of yourself that is completely peaceful and content. This is your basic self— secure and at ease.

You must allow this to happen, so that when distraction does come—and it will—you are better able to remain in the state of attentive awareness. When your mind is intensely paying attention to the focal point of your awareness, you open the door to the highest level of consciousness. This is the Creator energy, the place of highest power.

We all have the Creator energy within us. We do not always find access to it, simply because we do not always allow ourselves to truly focus on what we are doing and surrender to who we are. We allow distractions to sweep us away to the alternative possibilities that are constantly offering themselves, like forks in the road. That is the way in which brilliance is dulled into the mundane.

Deep awareness is the only skill necessary to create anything that is creatable, which of course is pretty much anything. When you invest your conscious awareness in an idea, the idea becomes enlivened with possibility. It begins to become real. Since you are spending time in the realm of consciousness that is this particular thought, you draw more connections to it, and begin to see ways to make it reality. This is true of things that you do not want, just as much as for things that you do want. You must be careful what you point your awareness toward. Fixating on the negative is the way that we bring it into being. There are consequences to our focus of attention.

The mind is not just a light that shines on the world; it affects the things it illuminates. The longer you look at a particular thing with your mind, the more you change it into the possibilities that occur to you as you observe it.

You change your world by looking.

You create your world by focusing.

Focus carefully.

Active Awareness

Moving from a place of helpless inaction to a place of inspired motion requires centered attention. This kind of mental skill must be cultivated. You do this by bringing your attention to a single-point of consciousness. When you drift away, you simply notice that you have lost focus, and bring yourself back to the state of awareness, the present moment, over and over again. This is the practice that brings us back to focus.

Described this way, the practice of focusing the mind—this repeated drifting away and calling ourselves back to the present moment— seems like work. It sounds unpleasant. It sounds like a losing battle. Fortunately, this is only one way to view the experience.

From the timeless perspective of consciousness, the mind does not blink. It does not waver. Consciousness is the connected moments of awareness that make up the gestalt of our attention. Time exists in our linear, subjective experience, but not in retrospect; a viewpoint that is just as valid when we construct our deeper understanding of what is. Knowledge of self comes from this place, and thus our awareness of the eternal moment called "focus" has no gaps, no cessation followed by reacquisition of focus. We are actually a collection of our moments of clarity, not a collection of our lapses in focus.

You are not your emptiness. You are not your chaos. You are the awareness that appears when your mind pays attention. You come to life when you generate consciousness through active awareness.

Therefore, it is impossible for you to lose focus. You only lose time. Of course, that is only true from the perspective of time. For when we remove time from the equation by looking holistically at our experience of awareness, we see that our consciousness is flawless. All we need to do is bring ourselves back whenever we realize that we have digressed.

In order to attain a deep understanding of something, or everything, all you have to do is keep bringing your awareness back to it. Eventually, you will see all its angles and understand it perfectly. The problem with humans is that we allow ourselves to become distracted and we stop processing, we stop engaging in the inquiry. If we take on the task of focusing more deeply and for longer periods of time, we can gain an infinite understanding about anything we choose to focus our attention upon.

Given this, the human mind has the potential for unwavering, perfect awareness. If you remove the remorse associated with the occasional breaks in attentiveness and heal them by removing the subjectivity and time, you begin to realize that we are all unlimited beings. We have everything within our grasp. We simply have thus far lacked the patience to implement this ability.

How do you begin to develop your powers of manifestation? Start with your ability to focus your mind. From this, you will learn who you are. When you get to the higher levels of this inquiry, you will discover that you are, at your most essential essence, the Champion of the Best-Case Scenario. When you realize that we all share the same goal in this regard, you will watch your ego to dissolve and you will be there; sharing the Universal Perspective with every saint, prophet and egoless proponent of humankind. You will be enlightened.

Begin with the simplest things: a blade of grass, a passing cloud, a tone in your mind. The specific subject of your awareness does not matter. Just put something in the middle of your mind and keep it there. When it disappears and is replaced by something else, bring your mind back to your original experience.

Yes, it is that simple.

Awakening into Purpose

You will come to a place
where your mind finally stops
and you begin to realize
your inner nature.

When this happens,
it is a true awakening.

Like all the Great Teachers of the past,
you will step into the light of who you really are.

When this happens
You will be awake.

🎱 Inspired Action

Your awakening will happen again and again, in a variety of contexts, as you awaken to what you truly represent and love. It happens when you discover your true purpose, which you have realized through this process of quieting your mind and listening for the answers from your higher self.

You are becoming larger with every epiphany that wakes you up to your true nature, which means that you are required to continually update your paradigm for who you think you are. This gives rise to true, authentic, novel purpose. When you act in the world committed to this end, you find that your life grows easier, like you are paddling downstream in the river of life.

This is called:
The Principle of Inspired Action:

"When you truly believe
in what you are doing,
you are far more likely to succeed."

When the object of your desire is pure in essence, and you have no guilt about what you are doing, things line up in favor of it coming into being. You must indulge yourself in things that have meaning to you, that give you joy on a deep level. By doing so you create effects, both tangible and quantum, that significantly increase the likelihood that you will succeed in doing whatever it is that you are striving to do.

This is one of the most empowering ideas that one can grasp, as it gives you the power to transform your life from an ordinary existence, devoid of true meaning, to one of higher causal vibration. Your power is based on your belief in what you are doing, and on the magnitude of positive emotion associated with your action. The better it feels, the higher the likelihood that it will succeed.

⛣ The Power of Meaning

In the course of our lives, most of us have repeatedly realized who we are and what we love. We have realized that we could be doing something more with our lives, something specific that has meaning to us. We have opened the door to the possibility that something wonderful can happen in our experience, something we no longer want to do without. Some of us have become so impassioned about this experience that, if we could no longer engage in this activity, we would find our life wholly intolerable.

When you know where you are going with your life—and you may have already realized it—the action of working to bring it about becomes your best source of life- energy. This is authentic inspiration, the highest form of happiness that an individual can experience. Following a path that is not inspired, not fully charged with meaning, can never result in an outcome that is as joyful and fulfilling. This is about choosing to have no other choice but the path of your inspiration, which turns out to be the very same path as the one that leads to happiness.

If you have realized who you are and what your gift to the world is, you must act on that realization. If you do not, you will die. Maybe not tomorrow, but eventually. In your final moments, you will have nothing else to do but reflect back on your experience here on earth.

Did you do what you came here to do? Did you realize something so true that you knew that your life, from that moment, was forever changed? Did you realize that from that point forward you had the possibility of being happier and more fulfilled than ever before? If you have experienced such an epiphany, you must do this thing, whatever it is, with the full force of your being. You must allow yourself to begin your new life starting right now.

You are not here to pick your nose, so to speak. The highest form of life begins with your choice to elaborate on a concept that is in complete alignment with your true being. All there really is to do in the universe is connect "who you really are" with "who you are being in your life right now." Anything else is just picking your nose.

You must act in order to become the physical, kinetic version of the person you have realized you are, the self that is the most meaningful expression of the highest plane of your thinking thus far. That may sound like a tall order, and it is. But if you don't ask the Big Questions, you don't get the Big Answers. These answers will shape who you become for the rest of your life.

Here is the question
we most need to repeatedly ask ourselves:

What is the highest expression of my true being?

You must ask yourself this question over and over. At different times in your life, you will get different answers to this question. Your life experiences will change the answers, because this is also a principle of the universe: Your truth will change.

Each moment of your existence, you are confronting a different set of circumstances. Each one has its own rules and governing dynamics. Nevertheless, your personal truth is real for you now. It will only make sense to you in the context of the life you are currently living.

When you are in contact with your highest purpose and the things that bring you the greatest joy, you will find that this is unchanging. This is the non-physical part of who you are before you had matter attached to you. These are the things that you know you will always be willing to say YES to. This is your true nature.

Nevertheless, you may still feel resistance to carrying out this expression of yourself. We all have fear and doubt. When we are in the world of motion, "real life" as it were, we will always have friction of some kind. Like an airplane flying through the atmosphere, drag will always be present. The way in which we reduce this drag is to notice that we have this internal resistance, and confront it directly. We notice that we are afraid to move forward, we notice why, and we move through it by acting deliberately in harmony with our original intention, in spite of the fear and doubt. In doing so we lean into our experience and surrender to being who we are.

You will awaken to the truth, and it will show you where to go and what to do. Your inner being knows the difference between right and wrong, just as it knows the difference between a constructive thought and a destructive one. Fear is simply a warning of danger, but it rarely tells us what we should do. It is merely trying to tell us what not to do, and when we need to pay attention. That does not mean that you should not proceed despite the fear. Fear is just another thought. When you realize that the thought that is in your head is taking you away from what you truly want, you must pay attention to whatever it is that you need to pay attention to, and then you must simply let it go. Dwelling on fear has no benefit.

The current content of your mind changes with every moment. If you do not like the way your thoughts feel to you or where they are leading, you need to take full responsibility for what is happening in your head.

Here is the abbreviated
Owner's Manual for the Mind:

If you do not like the thoughts
that are in your head,
they will remain,
until you change your mind.

Change them
before they change you.

Mental Training

If you try to do everything that inspires you, you will occasionally feel overwhelmed. This is the cost of an inspired life. You will have to confront the limiting thoughts that challenge your conviction, as well as take deliberate steps to prioritize the things that matter to you the most. If you want to cultivate the skill of letting go of thinking and reacquiring your connection to where you want to go in life, there simply is no more powerful way than meditation.

The word 'meditation' means many things, depending on whom you ask. What I mean here is that you must sit down, focus your mind, and listen for the answers—nothing more.

If you commit to spending fifteen minutes each day to remaining in the simple state of focus, you will have an easier time letting go of the thoughts that are not taking you toward who you truly want to be. You will be able to ask the important questions, and rather than forcing yourself to an immediate conclusion, you can take the more patient route of simply waiting for the answers. This is how you consult your higher self; your inner wisdom.

You need to sit and clear your head in the way a skydiver needs a parachute. This will allow you to get your life back under control by clearing your mind and allowing your original vision of who you are to return in its purest form.

You are created by thought. You life, with all of its exquisite details, is nothing more than the product of the magnetic quality of your own thinking. If you dare to dream big, in the direction that has meaning to you personally, you will be in the driver's seat of your life. You will be the pilot of a craft that is going exactly where you want it to go.

Can you imagine what the earth would be like if every human being lived this way? If you can imagine every man, woman and child taking the time to ask the important questions and sit down and listen for the answers, then you can begin to envision that all will in fact be well. As with everything, visualization is the beginning of creation.

This process begins with you. Each of us has to do this work on ourselves. We must all accept that we have a higher purpose, even if we have not yet realized it. When this pill is swallowed, there is a shift in consciousness that leads to more questions, and to more answers springing from inner wisdom. Believing in the possibility of a greater purpose is what awakens your connection to your higher self.

If you have not been engaging in this higher kind of thinking, do not fret. The way to begin is by realizing that you are never far from the all-important experience of appreciation, which can help you to love your life and the choices that have led up to the life you are living now. When you get into this headspace, you will be able to open yourself to a higher vision of who you can be.

The future is limited only by your own vision. If you have not arrived at a place of profound experience, it is ultimately because of choices you have made in your daily life. Have you chosen to meditate today? Have you done something that inspires you? Have you taken a moment to open yourself up to greater possibilities than the ones you have conceived thus far?

When you ask these kinds of questions, you are igniting new thoughts and new realms of experience. This is the only way to reach down into yourself to bring out what is there. It is this profound sense of self that drives you forward into a reality that resonates with who you truly are, rather than one that you receive as a victim of life's momentum.

Of course, in reality there are no victims. There are simply those who have been creating more with their negative thinking than their powers of purposeful creation. People who lead happy lives are the ones who, on some level, have come to understand the profound concept of the magnetic attraction of thinking. When we think about something repeatedly, we draw it to us. Like a magnet, we bring into our reality experiences that resemble the nature of that which we hold in our minds.

This makes perfect sense when we consider the positive method of creation. When we dream a dream and give ourselves permission to allow it to happen, it will happen. You must believe in the dream with all of your being, but if are truly ready for success it can occur. Proof of this can be seen in the lives of successful people everywhere. They have a vision that they believe in, and they take all the necessary steps to make their vision a reality, the most important of which is to continually believe that it is going to become real. That's the part that most of us get stuck on.

There is another way to create as well, one that involves the mirror image of this way of bringing into the world that which we hold in our minds. When we have a thought that creates a feeling that is the opposite of to who we want to be or where we want to go, we find ourselves dwelling upon this thought. Believing that we are working toward preventing whatever it is from happening; we focus upon the thing that we wish to avoid. This kind of focusing has just as much power to create as dwelling on the vision of what we desire. Simply because we have focused our minds upon it, instead of focusing our creative energy on what we want as an alternative, we find that we bring about the experience we were hoping to avoid.

The emotional thought that appears as a warning is important. It is a navigational aid, which comes from a place in yourself that speaks to you in feelings, not words. This is your inner self, sending you important messages about your true nature. When you take these messages and focus entirely upon them, however, you are not working to create in the world that you do want so dearly to unfold.

We wake up and there are a finite number of minutes ahead of us in the day, and months in the year. If we spend all of our time dwelling on the "no's," we are not engaged in the act of conscious creation. We are simply shouting to the universe what we are focused upon, and the universe responds by giving us exactly that.

When we think thoughts like, "I do not want to run out of money," the universe hears, "I want to run out of money," and so we find ourselves running low on money. This happens, first, because we are not envisioning what it would be like to be financially comfortable, and, second, because we are not engaged in the process of asking specifically how we can bring more capital into our lives. We are not solving the problem; we are simply focusing on it and giving it energy.

In order to walk the path of deliberate construction of our lives, we need to recognize that our thoughts have weight. The more we think a thought, the more mass it has. As a freight train is hard to stop because of its weight, a persistent thought has ways of producing more embodiments of its own tone and nature.

Emotion is what ties our thoughts together and gives them power. The feeling behind our thinking, whether it is happy or sad, is the climate in which our thoughts are born. If we choose to keep our internal climate joyful and full of zest for life, we will bring into our experience things that will create more of this emotion.

The choice to be happy is your own. No one has to teach you this skill; you already know how to do it. You were born with this knowledge. You must remember how to transcend your current state of affairs, your present predicaments, and maintain a sense of joyful appreciation for what you have and where you are going. Further, you must choose to remember and accept that who you are is someone that you admire and enjoy.

You know how to have a good time. You know what makes you happy, and it is unique to you. If you can tap into this feeling right now, you will understand that it is this sensation that can help you to manifest more experiences that create the same feeling. When you are feeling good you inevitably find yourself becoming filled with possibilities of other things that will feel just as good. Joy creates more joy.

This can pertain to your recreation, but it can also invade every other experience in your life. Whatever you are doing, do it with a sense of delight. This will lead you to success in that specific matter, which will bring about a continued feeling of happiness. From there, you simply foster this vibration and allow it to infiltrate every aspect of your existence.

You are in a process of becoming you. As your experiences accumulate, you learn what you *do not* desire, just as much as you learn what you *do* wish for. These experiences and thoughts continue to shape your sense of self. Day by day, this process of comparison and contrast guides you to become more and more aware of you are who you really are.

By focusing on your failures and shortcomings, you can easily get lost in the negative perspective and forget that there is another side of the coin. True, you are a collection of your errors. That is how you came to learn who you do not want to be and what you do not want to do. But you are also a collection of your beauty as well, and of the times you revealed truly beautiful character. This version of you has its own inertia too, and will continue to manifest itself on into the future.

If you want to continue progressing in the direction of your highest vision for yourself as an embodiment of your ideals, you must get your thinking under control. When you realize that you are thinking in a negative manner out of habit, you must immediately and firmly choose to draw your attention toward that which you want to be. This is totally your responsibility.

This is not going to happen in a day. Do not let that bother you. Every sentient being has past habits from which they are recovering. If you dwell on this, you are perpetuating the cycle of thinking that you wish to break out of. You have been operating your mind in the way that you have been operating it for a very long time. It will require time to change that. You will, however, begin the process of waking up earlier and earlier as you become steadfast in your resolve to do what feels good to you on a deep level.

Your feelings are your guide, and they are at the heart of your power to create. Pushing them away is a trap that we sometimes find ourselves in. When we find ourselves feeling good, we strive remain in this state at all times, at any cost. This can lead us to lose the muscle of our emotionally charged intent.

If you are really onto something, it will come into your consciousness with feeling. The stronger your conviction, the more powerful the feeling will be. These feelings push us out of the comfort zones in our lives, and allow us to step forward into the scary and challenging realm of inspired action.

Sometimes this emotional tone is pleasurable; sometimes it is not. Whatever it is, the emotion marks your path. One way or another, you must walk this path if you are to carry out that which your gut is telling you to do.

Everyone likes to feel good. At times, however, you will find that your path brings you up against something profoundly distasteful, and anger is the appropriate emotion. If you convince yourself to calm down and let go of your negative feeling without examining the message, you will be missing an essential piece of information about who you are in this particular situation.

If we take a lesson from the ancient Aikido masters, we must remain in connection to the energy, no matter what it is and where it is going. Once we marry into this relationship, we can then fearlessly guide things away from a direction we think of as "bad", toward an outcome that we believe is "good". This is the only way to control the world. Purchase into the relationship, define yourself as a part of it, and you have the power to create change.

Regaining Perspective

No matter where you are in your life, there is a higher perspective from which to see your situation. If you allow yourself to do so, you can feel appreciation for the specific nature of your life. You have attracted what is happening, one way or another. If you look at it from the perspective of creation, you were the All-Powerful Being that was afforded the freedom to make it unfold as it did.

This may not be easy for you to accept at first. Most of us begin from a place of uncertainty. You may have been feeling like the receiver of your experience, rather than the creator of it. The truth is, we all start from that feeling. That's the culture that many of us were brought up in: "life stinks, get used to it." But this is completely irrelevant to our future, however, since we can shed anything we want to, simply by focusing on where we want to go rather than on where we have been.

When you start down the path of purposefully creating your life, you will feel more effective as the chooser of your life experience simply because you are witness to the magical process of manifestation through thought. You have actually seen it work, and seeing is believing.

This cannot happen until you decide what is right for you, which is something you need to realize with your emotional center. When you connect with true passion, it will guide you toward a truer understanding of what it is that you want. From there, all you need to do is invent what you want in your head, and actually believe it is going to happen. Of course, that requires you to let go of your guilt about your success.

Your life will flow better when you choose to invest yourself in what you know to be the right thing for you. When you focus on creating experiences that, beyond being the right thing for you, are also the right thing for the people around you, things flow even easier. That is when you kick your life into high gear. When the thing that you have chosen to invest your energy in is good for all those concerned, you are connected to the source of all energy.

There is nothing that lights up a life more than an idea whose time has come; an idea that others will agree with. If the idea helps others, it is far more likely to succeed than an idea whose sole beneficiary is you.

This is the age-old secret called:

Mutual Benefit

When you are helping others with the dream you have chosen to make into reality, you are certain to fall in love with what you are doing. The sheer profundity of the concept fills your actions with meaning, and you cannot fail. You may not create exactly what you originally envisioned. You will, however, be more likely to manifest the general principle of your dream, simply because it is *something worth attaining.* You are fighting on the right side, on the side of the common good. No matter how things turn out, you will find fulfillment, simply because you like who you are.

Despite appearances, we usually end up improving things on a larger scale than we realize. Even when our actions appear insignificant in the overall scheme of things, every little bit helps. Even when you believe that you are wasting your time, that your life doesn't mean much, you have the potential to make a huge difference in the world around you.

If you work in a highway tollbooth you can smile at the toll-payers.

If you are a toll-payer you can smile at the tollbooth operator.

A mere candle is enough to light up a dark room.

It isn't that hard. The simple act of shining a genuine smile at a stranger gives them the hope that things are going to be OK in the world. If a complete stranger is unafraid of human contact, and takes the chance to pass on good vibes, we might actually be living in "Good Times." Remember, good feelings are every bit as contagious as bad feelings.

Imagine what it would be like if we were all in a good mood at the same time. Imagine that each stranger who crosses your path smiles at you simply because they are having a great life at this moment, and they wanted to share the good feeling.

Imagine that.

If we don't all conceive of this possibility, it cannot come to pass. If, on the other hand, we entertain this vision, this dream of "Good Times" will grow in probability until one day, when our resistance is gone, it will actually happen. Let it be.

We must pass on the good feelings when we have them, and infuse our actions with genuine liveliness, fueled by our belief in who we are and in what we are doing with our lives. This will act like an energy magnifier that will bring about a higher level of evolution in our lives. If we all live that way, it will inevitably bring about the next phase in of the evolution of civilization on earth.

We must all pull together to make this happen.

...and we will.

Afterword

To my brothers and sisters of the human race:

May your journey lead you to water,
and everything else that allows you
to continue your trip on a good note.

Please take care of each other.

When you are ready

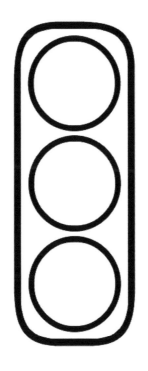

color the light green.